THE
HUMAN BODY

Barbara A. Somervill
Contributing author: Carol Ryback
Consultant: Suzy Gazlay, M.A.,
science curriculum resource teacher

Please visit our web site at: www.garethstevens.com
For a free color catalog describing Gareth Stevens Publishing's list
of high-quality books, call 1-800-542-2595 (USA)
or 1-800-387-3178 (Canada).

Library of Congress Cataloging-in-Publication Data

Somervill, Barbara A.
    The human body / Barbara Somervill. — North American ed.
        p. cm. — (Gareth Stevens Vital Science: Life Science)
    Includes bibliographical references and index.
    ISBN-13: 978-0-8368-8441-8 — ISBN-10: 0-8368-8441-8 (lib. bdg.)
    ISBN-13: 978-0-8368-8450-0 — ISBN-10: 0-8368-8450-7 (softcover)
    1. Body, Human. 2. Human physiology. I. Title.
    QP37.S724   2008
    612—dc22   2007016175

This edition first published in 2008 by
Gareth Stevens Publishing
A Weekly Reader® Company
1 Reader's Digest Road
Pleasantville, NY 10570-7000 USA

Q2a Media editor: Honor Head
Q2a Media design, illustrations, and image research: Q2a Media
Q2a Media cover design: Q2a Media

Gareth Stevens editor: Carol Ryback
Gareth Stevens art direction: Tammy West
Gareth Stevens graphic designer: Dave Kowalski
Gareth Stevens production: Jessica Yanke
Gareth Stevens science curriculum consultant: Suzy Gazlay, M.A.

Photo credits: t=top, b=bottom, m=middle, l=left, r=right
All photographs by Darren Sawyer (www.sawyersphoto.com)
Anatomical Travelogue / Science Photo Library: 9. Science Photo Library: / John Daugherty 11(bl).
Photolibrary: / Photo Researchers, Inc. 11(br). Photolibrary: / Phototake Inc. 13, 23(bl), 41.
Photolibrary: / Science Photo Library 17(b), 29, 33, 34(tl), 37(tl), 42, 43. CORBIS: / Matthias Kulka
19, 21; / Michael Freeman 36(bl). iStockphoto: / Linda Bucklin 23(tr); / Peter Galbraith 25.
Photolibrary: / BSIP 26(tl).

Printed in the United States of America

1 2 3 4 5 6 7 8 9 11 10 09 08 07

Contents

The Basis of Life: From Elements to DNA

All matter—living or not—is made up of elements. In the human body, varying quantities of different elements combine to make us what we are. About 93 percent of a typical human body consists of three elements—oxygen, carbon, and hydrogen. Our bodies also contain trace amounts of many other elements, including cobalt, beryllium, and radium. Chemical analysis of a human body reveals tiny amounts of elements that are poisonous in large quantities, such as arsenic, mercury, and lead. Your body stays healthy by maintaining a balance of all of its elements.

The body of an adult who weighs 150 pounds (70 kilograms) contains about 10 gallons (38 liters) of water.

The molecular structure of DNA is similar to a twisting ladder. DNA holds the blueprint to life.

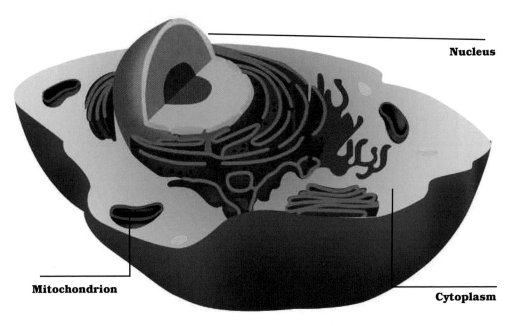

Nucleus

Mitochondrion

Cytoplasm

The different parts of a cell work together to support life.

That person also carries around 44 pounds (20 kg) of carbon and about 3.3 pounds (1.5 kg) of lime (calcium oxide). Water, carbon, and calcium within a human body look nothing like puddles, lumps of coal, or garden fertilizer. Instead, these and other elements form the cells that make up our body parts and organs.

Units of Life

Your ten trillion cells are the basic working units of life. In humans, as in all animals, a cell membrane encloses the main portion of the cell, called the cytoplasm. This gel-like substance contains smaller cell parts—the organelles—including the nucleus, which controls the workings of each cell. Every cell organelle performs a specific job. For example, mitochondria convert food to energy, and lysosomes dispose of damaged cells. Although each cell contains basically the same parts, the cells within the body can differ greatly.

The cell's nucleus contains lumps of loosely arranged material called chromatin. Chromatin is made of protein and deoxyribonucleic acid, better known as DNA. During human cell division, the chromatin becomes orderly, forming twenty-three pairs of chromosomes—rod-shaped structures of DNA. The DNA carries genetic material, usually called the genes.

30,000 Genes

Nearly every cell in the human body contains about 30,000 genes. These carry the instructions that the body follows to create a unique person. Genes determine the sex, height, eye color, bone structure, and thousands of

Genetics Milestone

In 1953, scientists James Watson of the U.S. and Francis Crick of England determined that DNA has a double helix shape—it looks like a twisted ladder.

other details that make each person different.

Half of our genes come from our mother and half from our father. This explains why you might have your mother's nose, your father's bright blue eyes, the curly hair of your mother's mother, the musical talent of your dad's father, and great-grandma's smile. As you can see, every person is a genetic mixture.

Pronunciation Key:

cytoplasm (SIGH-toh-plaz-em)
mitochondria
(migh-toh-KHAN-dree-uh)
deoxyribonucleic
(dee-AHK-see-RYE-boh-new-KLEE-ick)

7

2 The Respiratory System

Breathe in . . . breathe out . . . breathe in . . . breathe out. We normally inhale and exhale automatically in a smooth, rhythmic pattern. You usually do not think about each breath, you just breathe. Sitting quietly, you will exchange about 1.5 gallons (6 liters) of air per minute.

The respiratory system brings oxygen into the body and removes carbon dioxide, a waste gas produced by metabolic processes of the body. Respiration begins at your nose, where air enters. Nose hairs filter out dirt, dust, and bacteria. Nasal passages warm and moisten the inhaled air.

Warmed, wet air travels down to the pharynx and larynx. The pharynx, better known as the

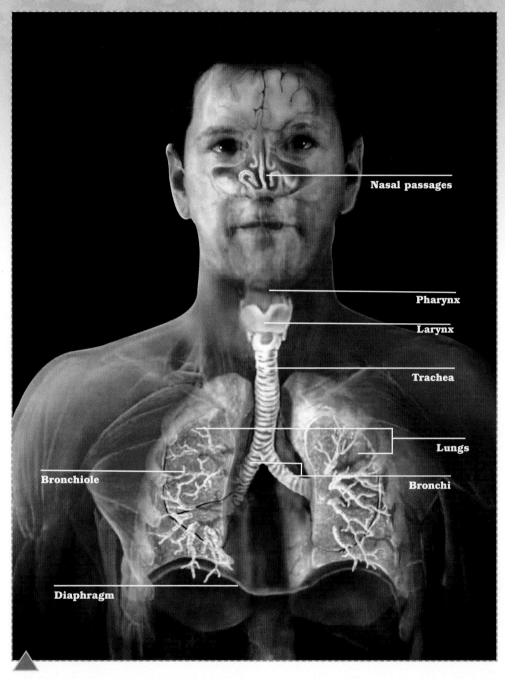

Nasal passages

Pharynx

Larynx

Trachea

Lungs

Bronchiole

Bronchi

Diaphragm

The respiratory system is a complex network of passages that take in oxygen and get rid of the body's gaseous wastes.

throat, funnels air into the larynx, or voice box. The larynx is made of cartilage (a flexible connective tissue), mucous membranes, and muscles. As air enters the larynx, it passes over the vocal folds, which vibrate when we speak, scream, or cry.

A flap of tissue called the epiglottis flips over the top of the larynx as we swallow. The epiglottis keeps food and liquids out of the larynx.

Air moves from the larynx into the trachea, or windpipe. In most adults, the trachea measures nearly 5 inches (12 centimeters) long and 1 inch (2.5 cm) wide. The trachea is kept open by incomplete rings of cartilage.

Miles of Airways

Adult human lungs contain about 1,500 miles (2,400 km) of airways and, on average, about 480 million alveoli.

From the trachea, air moves into the bronchi, two tubes leading to each lung. The bronchi then branch off into numerous tiny tubes, called bronchioles. Every bronchiole leads to even smaller air chambers, called alveoli, deep in the lungs.

Alveoli resemble miniature grape clusters. The alveoli walls are thin—only one cell thick—and form the inner lining of the lungs. This is where the blood swaps its carbon dioxide for oxygen.

Lungs

The lungs lie in the chest on either side of the heart. The right lung has three lobes, while the left has only two. The smaller left lung allows room in the chest for the heart.

Blood traveling through our bodies enters our lung tissue and eventually passes through the tiniest of all blood vessels, called capillaries. Like the alveoli, the walls of the capillaries are also only one

alveoli *(al-VE-o-lie)*
bronchi *(BRAHN-kigh)*
emphysema *(em-fi-ZEE-ma)*
larynx *(LAHR-inks)*
pharynx *(FAHR-inks)*
trachea *(TRAY-kee-uh)*

cell thick. This allows for the instantaneous exchange of waste carbon dioxide gas for oxygen. So, the purplish blood loaded with carbon dioxide that enters the lungs leaves as bright red, oxygen-rich blood. This exchange occurs about twelve times a minute—every minute of every day of your life.

A flat, thick muscle, called the diaphragm, lies directly below the lungs. It helps force air in and out of the body. Nerves connected to the brain signal the lungs to take a breath. Ribs, which form a protective cage around the lungs, are made partly of cartilage. The cartilage allows your chest to expand and contract as the lungs inhale and exhale air.

A damaged respiratory system affects the entire body. When the continuous exchange of oxygen for carbon dioxide cannot happen, illness results. For instance, years of smoking breaks down the thin, fragile walls of the alveoli. Large air pockets develop in the lungs. The person constantly feels the need to breathe out. This incurable disease is called emphysema.

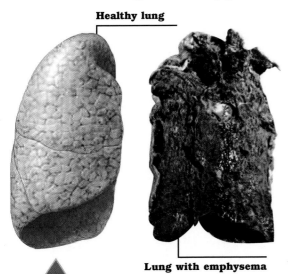

Healthy lung

Lung with emphysema

Emphysema does long-term damage to otherwise healthy lungs.

3 The Circulatory System

The circulatory system is a blood transportation network that reaches every part of the body. It includes the blood, a pump (the heart), and a series of vessels through which the blood flows. Those vessels include veins, arteries, and capillaries.

The heart is a four-chambered organ that pumps blood throughout the body. Most adult-sized bodies have about 1.3 gallons (5 l) of blood. The average human heart weighs roughly 11 ounces (300 grams)—less than 1 pound (454 g). As you grow, your heart is always about the size of your fist.

The heart is located between the lungs in the chest, or thoracic, cavity. The heart is wider at the top and contains two chambers called

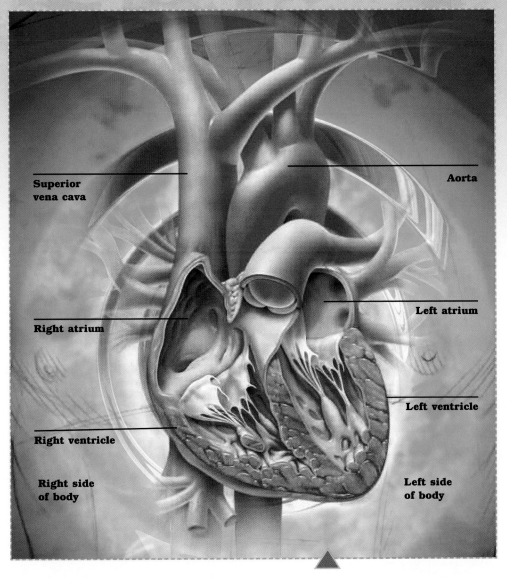

Superior
vena cava

Aorta

Right atrium

Left atrium

Right ventricle

Left ventricle

Right side
of body

Left side
of body

the left and right atria (singular:
atrium). The lower, pointy part
of the heart also contains two
chambers, called the left and
right ventricles.

A normal heart beats about
72 to 75 times every minute. In
an average 75-year lifespan, a heart

*The average heart beats
about three billion times
in a person's lifetime.*

Pronunciation Key:

antigens *(AN-tih-jenz)*
aorta *(ay-OR-tuh)*
atria *(AY-tree-uh)*
thoracic *(thuh-RASS-ick)*
ventricle *(VEHN-trih-cle)*

will beat about 3 billion times. The heart constantly moves blood, so the circulatory system has no beginning or end. Blood arriving at the heart enters the right atrium. As the heart muscle contracts ("beats"), blood moves into the right ventricle. Another heartbeat sends that blood to the lungs.

Oxygenated blood from the lungs returns to the heart. It enters the left atrium. Another heartbeat sends the blood into the left ventricle. The left ventricle's powerful contraction pulses the blood to the rest of the body.

Blood Vessels

Blood leaves the heart through the aorta, the largest artery in the body. Blood flows at about 16 feet (5 meters) per second through the aorta.

Arteries are blood vessels that carry oxygen-rich blood away from the heart. From the aorta, blood travels through a network of smaller arteries. It finally enters the capillaries, the tiniest of all blood vessels. Capillaries deliver oxygen and nutrients to human tissues.

Capillaries can also act as veins to carry blood back toward the heart. Tissue capillaries feed into small veins, which connect into increasingly larger veins. Veins have valves that prevent blood from flowing backward. This is particularly important with leg veins that carry large volumes of blood. The largest vein is the superior vena cava. It empties into the right atrium.

Blood is like a river of life that travels throughout the body. In addition to oxygen, the blood also absorbs water and nutrients through the vessels of the digestive system and delivers them to the rest of the body for use. Waste products are filtered from the blood by various tissues. For instance, the kidneys filter excess water and waste chemicals to the bladder for removal from the body.

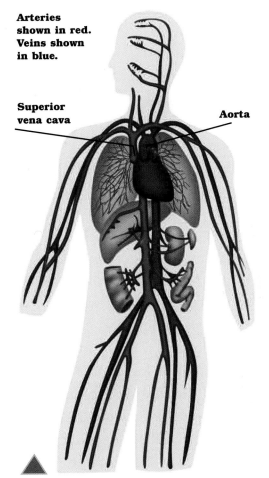

Arteries shown in red. Veins shown in blue.

Superior vena cava

Aorta

Arteries carry blood away from the heart. Veins carry blood to the heart.

Blood also carries hormones through the body. Hormones are liquid chemical messengers that help body organs adjust to conditions within the body.

Blood

Blood is composed of red blood cells, white blood cells, platelets, and plasma. About 55 percent of the total volume of blood is plasma, the straw-colored fluid portion of blood. Red blood cells (RBCs) make up roughly 45 percent of blood volume, and white blood cells (WBCs) account for about 1 percent. Our blood looks red because of red blood cells.

New Red Cells

Red blood cells carry oxygen. Your body is constantly producing new RBCs. Each red blood cell only lasts about 120 days. New RBCs are produced in bone marrow at a rate of two million every second. As red blood cells wear out, the spleen removes them from circulation.

White blood cells guard the body and help it heal. They fight off viruses and bacteria that cause infection. When an infection occurs, WBCs collect at the site and attack the invading organisms.

Platelets are tiny cell fragments that promote blood clotting. Capillaries are constantly breaking apart. If blood couldn't clot, people would bleed to death within their bodies. Clotting seals cuts and prevents blood from oozing out of body tissues.

William Harvey
(1578–1657)

British doctor William Harvey researched the pathways of the vessels that lead to and from the heart and came up with the idea of the circulatory system. Harvey experimented on small animals to prove that blood passes from the veins to the right side of the heart.

A black-and-blue mark, or bruise, on your skin is a sign that minor blood vessels were damaged. A bruise is clotted blood under the skin.

Types of Blood

Blood is divided into four basic types: A, B, AB, and O. The letters refer to the antigens within the blood. An antigen is a molecule in the blood whose shape triggers a response by the immune system. Blood types are further classified into positive (having antigens) and negative (not having antigens).

Knowing a person's blood type is important when a blood transfusion is required. Ideally, in a blood transfusion, the donor and the recipient have the same blood type.

Generally, a person with A-negative blood cannot receive blood from a person with B-positive blood. The A-negative blood "sees" the new blood as an invader, like an infection, and destroys it. Someone with O-negative blood, however, can donate blood to anyone. People with type AB-positive can receive any blood type. Medical personnel do not like to make such substitutions, however.

Lymphatic System

The human body contains another system of vessels—the lymphatic system. This network includes lymphatic vessels, lymph nodes, the spleen, and bone marrow.

The lymphatic system is part of the immune system, which helps keep the body healthy. Lymph nodes act as guard posts to prevent infection from moving through the body.

Lymph is a clear, yellowish, watery liquid that contains white blood cells. It circulates through the lymphatic vessels, a network of vessels that

Hard-working Hearts

A heart pumps 2,000 gallons (7,570 liters) of blood a day.

weaves throughout the body, often alongside the circulatory system's vessels. Unlike blood, fluid in the lymph system flows in only one direction. Multiple valves inside the lymph vessels prevent backward flow.

Lymph removes bacteria and unwanted proteins from tissues. It also carries fats from the small intestine and releases cells that fight diseases. Many of these disease-fighting cells are produced in the spleen. Lymph empties into the bloodstream through two main lymphatic ducts.

Dr. William Harvey researched the circulatory system.

4 The Skeletal System

Human bones form a skeleton. The word comes from the Greek *skeletos*, meaning "dried up." Our skeleton provides a framework for muscles, blood vessels, organs, and nerves.

Bones give us strength, structure, and protection. The skull and spine protect the brain and spinal cord. Ribs offer a flexible support that allows us to breathe.

Bone marrow deep inside our long and flat bones produces red blood cells. Bones also serve as storage areas for minerals used by the body.

Most people do not have a good understanding of what bones are like. They think bones are dry, hard, and solid. Bones are not dry. If a bone is cut, it bleeds.

Growing Bones

Bones have two major growth periods—during infancy and during puberty, or adolescence.

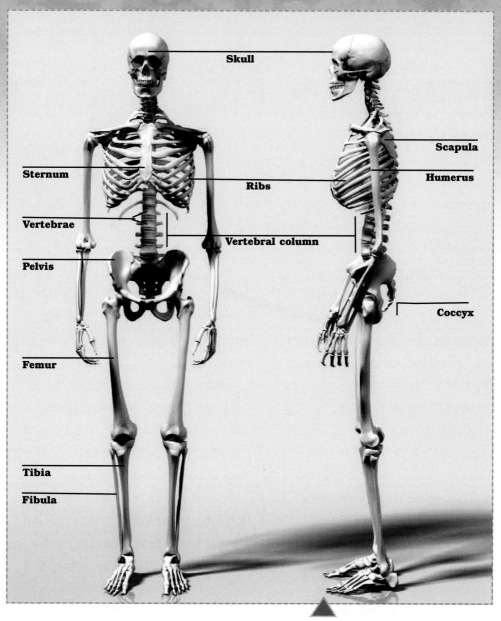

Skull

Scapula

Sternum

Humerus

Ribs

Vertebrae

Vertebral column

Pelvis

Coccyx

Femur

Tibia

Fibula

Bones are also not completely solid. While they may seem hard, bones can and do break. Most bone segments have cylinder-shaped tunnels that allow blood vessels to pass through them, while the insides

The skeleton supports the muscles and other soft tissues of the human body.

of others resemble a lacy honeycomb of bone matter. Bones grow, change, and renew themselves continuously.

Bone matter may be compact or spongy. Eighty percent of all bone is compact (cortical) bone. This type of bone forms in a circular pattern around a central cylinder. Blood vessels pass through the central, tunnel-like section. Compact bone is found in the long bones such as the tibia or femur.

Spongy bone is a delicate, lacy honeycomb of bone. This type of bone is found in the vertebrae, ribs, and pelvis. Although spongy bone is lighter in weight than compact bone, it is remarkably strong.

Bones are made of calcium phosphate. They often contain trace amounts of sodium, magnesium, and zinc. An adult human body contains about 206 bones in a variety of shapes and sizes. Long

 Pronunciation Key:

coccyx *(CAHK-six)*
humerus *(HYOO-muhr-us)*
sacral *(SAY-kruhl)*
vertebral *(ver-TEE-bruhl)*

bones, such as the femur, tibia, and humerus, are found in legs and arms. Long bones have a standard "dogbone" shape—a long shaft with rounded, knobby ends. Flat bones, found in the skull, pelvis (hips), and scapula (shoulder blades), are thinner and mostly flat.

Our genes generally determine the length, strength, and mass of our bones. Good bones are programmed into our DNA. Nutrition and personal activity also affect our bone structure. Strong bones need calcium, protein, and a variety of vitamins on a regular basis.

Although weak stomach muscles cause many back problems, poor nutrition, bad posture, and carrying heavy loads can create long-term skeletal problems.

The Body's Midline

Skeletal system bones usually come in pairs, one for each side of the body. For example, a body has two tibias (one in each leg) and two sets of ribs (one on each side of the body). Bones along the midline of the body do not have duplicates. These include the skull, the vertebral column, and the sternum (breastbone).

A newborn's skull is not one unit but several soft, loose, floating plates. The skull's plates must squeeze together during birth so the baby's head has an easier time leaving its mother's body. During early childhood, the skull continues to grow, slowly binding itself into a solid bone structure.

The skull fits on top of the vertebral column—a stack

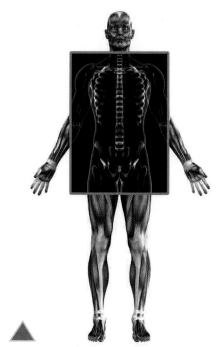

A fluoroscope shows bones beneath muscles and organs.

An Accidental Invention

In 1895, researcher Wilhelm Roentgen investigated invisible rays. He accidently placed his hand in the path of those rays and an image of his hand appeared on the screen behind him. This accident led to the discovery of X-rays. Modern medical facilities use X-rays in a variety of ways.

of 33 bones in children (26 bones in adults). The vertebral column is often referred to as the backbone, or spine. The vertebral column ends at the tailbone.

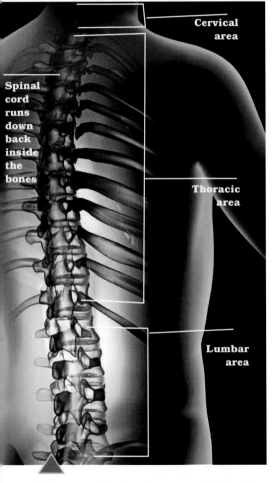

Cervical area

Spinal cord runs down back inside the bones

Thoracic area

Lumbar area

The vertebral column protects the spinal cord, which carries nerve signals from the brain to the rest of the body.

Each vertebra is a separate bone that surrounds the spinal cord, the main portion of the nervous system. The vertebral column is divided into five sections. The neck (cervical) segment contains seven bones. The chest (thoracic) segment has twelve bones, mostly attached to the ribs. Five vertebrae form the small of the back, called the lumbar section.

In an adult, two fused (joined) segments of five bones form the sacral region. The coccyx, or tailbone—which was once four small bones— makes up the lowest part of the spine.

Joints

Bones connect to each other at joints. Some joints, such as those found along seams in the skull, are fixed joints. They do not bend. These skull joints form along irregular lines called sutures.

Other joints allow bones to move either in a back-and-forth or a rotating motion. Moveable joints have four main designs:

• Hinge joints (elbows, knees, and fingers) allow a back-and-forth movement in a straight line.

• Pivot joints (at the top of the vertebral column) allow the head to move up and down as well as side to side.

• Ball-and-socket joints (hips and shoulders) allow the greatest range of motion. Ball-and-socket joints allow limbs to rotate in a full circle.

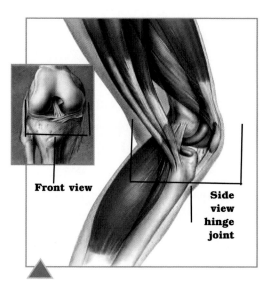

Front view

Side view hinge joint

A knee is an example of a hinge joint. It allows the lower leg to swing back and forth.

• Gliding joints (base of the spine and wrist) allow bones to slide over each other.

Joints allow the body to move smoothly. Certain joints contain bone-to-bone connections, called ligaments.

Weight-bearing joints have natural shock absorbers. In the spine, cartilaginous disks separate and cushion vertebrae. The disks keep vertebrae from grinding on each other. A disk that slips out of place because of injury or accident causes great pain. Bursas—fluid-filled sacs that act as cushions—pad knee, hip, and shoulder joints.

Tendon and Ligaments

Tendons connect muscles to bones or to other muscles. They help give a flexed muscle a rounded shape. Tendons act much like rubber bands of tissue that help bones move.

Ligaments attach bone to bone or other organs. They hold bones together to form a more stable joint.

5 The Muscular System

Muscles have many functions in the human body. They help us stand, sit, and walk. They move food through our bodies and push air in and out. Muscles are long strips of tissue covering our bones, organs, and joints. They allow us to smile, wink, and frown. Our muscles are specialized into three main cell types. We have skeletal, smooth, and cardiac muscle cells. We can control only the skeletal muscles.

Skeletal (striated) muscles attach to the skeleton. They wrap around or over bones and joints. Control of these muscles is voluntary—we choose to make an arm or leg move. Large movements, such as walking and running, and small movements, such as writing or knitting, depend

*Skeletal muscles work in groups to
allow the body to bend, stretch, walk,
run, sit, and stand.*

Careers in Sports Medicine

Sports medicine techniques can also help nonathletes.

Sports medicine specialists deal with concerns that affect an athlete's performance. They stress the importance of strength and endurance training, proper nutrition, bone and joint health and repair, and cardiac (heart) health. The sports medicine career field include doctors, physical therapists, personal trainers, and nutritionists.

on clusters of muscle cells working together. A skeletal muscle, such as the biceps found in the upper arm, may have one hundred thousand cells. Skeletal muscles can be trained to increase personal strength and speed.

Skeletal muscles work in pairs. One set of muscles flexes (bends) an arm and another set returns the arm to its original position. A muscle can only contract to pull on bones. Muscles do not push bones. For instance, your biceps muscle contracts to bend your fist toward your shoulder. Your triceps muscle contracts when you straighten your arm.

An action that requires complicated movements uses a larger number of muscles. Our faces, for example, have many muscle sets that raise eyebrows, blink, talk, smile, frown, and kiss. The strongest facial muscles are four pairs of powerful muscles that move the jaw and allow us to chew.

Pronunciation Key:

esophagus *(eh-SAH-fa-gus)*
ligament *(LI-guh-ment)*
peristalsis *(pear-ih-STAHL-sis)*
skeletal *(SKEH-leh-tuhl)*

Smooth Muscles

Smooth muscles are found in the walls of hollow body organs, such as the bladder, intestines, and blood vessels.

Smooth muscle cells are spindle-shaped. They often form into layered sheets of muscle that appear in organ walls. These layered muscle sheets are set at different angles to one another and contract at different times. Smooth muscles contract slowly and rest between contractions.

We do not control smooth muscles. They work on their own. For example, after we swallow food, it passes into the pharynx and esophagus. Involuntary (smooth) muscles take over. They rhythmically contract to push food down the esophagus into the stomach. In the stomach, layers of smooth muscle contract to mix and break down food. This smooth muscle action of the digestive tract is called peristalsis. It also moves material through the intestines.

Cardiac Muscle

Cardiac (heart) muscle works automatically. An adult human heart beats, or contracts, at a rate of one beat in less than a second.

A resting heart pumps about 1.3 gallons (5 l) of blood a minute. During heavy exercise, blood flow may increase to five times that amount—about 6.5 gallons (25 l) per minute—to supply more oxygen to the skeletal muscles. Digestion slows down.

When we sleep, the heart beats much slower. Unlike skeletal muscles, the heart cannot rest for hours at a time. It rests between beats.

6 Processing Food, Water, and Waste

The body is a machine. Every day, it requires fuel in the form of food and water. Solid and liquid nourishment enters the body through the mouth. The digestive system processes this fuel. It extracts and absorbs vitamins, minerals, and other nutrients from our food and fluid intake—which creates liquid and solid wastes. The excretory system rids the body of these waste products.

The Gastrointestinal System

The digestive system is made up of two main parts: the gastrointestinal tract and accessory organs. Digestion begins in the mouth. Adult humans have up to thirty-two teeth that bite, tear, and grind food. As the teeth chew food, salivary glands in the

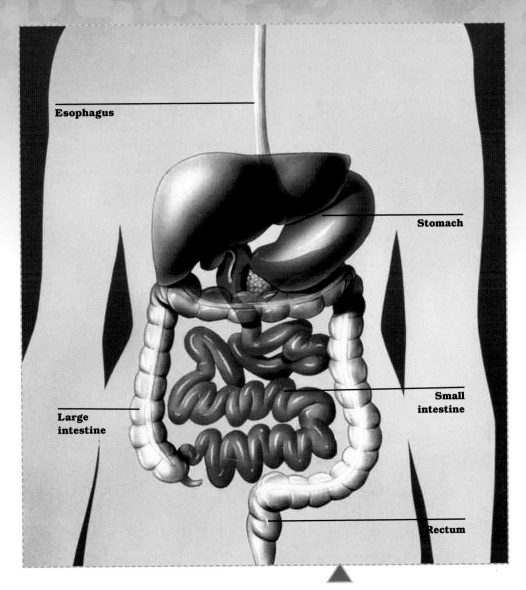

Esophagus

Stomach

Large
intestine

Small
intestine

Rectum

cheeks and the floor of the mouth release saliva. The saliva mixes with the chewed food to help form a ball that can be swallowed easily.

The tongue is a muscular flap that moves food around in the mouth. It is sensitive to hot and cold. About ten thousand taste

As food moves through the digestive tract, the body absorbs the nutrients it needs.

buds on the tongue help us enjoy sweet, tart, salty, and sour food. The tongue also forces food to the back of the mouth so it can be swallowed.

Food moves down the pharynx to the esophagus, a 10-inch (25-cm) muscular tube connected to the stomach.

The stomach, a storage tank for food and liquids, is made of three layers of strong, smooth muscles. As these muscles squeeze and churn the stomach, gastric juices mix with its contents to turn food into a usable mash. Gastric juices include enzymes, acid, and mucus. The enzymes and acid break down food particles. The mucus protects the stomach lining from the acids.

Intestines

From the stomach, liquefied food enters the small intestine. The small intestine gets its name from its narrow diameter. With an overall length of more than 20 feet

 Pronunciation Key:

cecum (SEE-kum)

duodenum (do-uh-DEE-num)

excretory (EK-skra-tor-ee)

gastrointestinal (GAS-troh-in-TESS-ti-nuhl)

ileum (IH-lee-uhm)

jejunum (ji-JOO-num)

(6 m), it is more than three times as long as the large intestine.

The first section of the small intestine, the duodenum, is about 12 inches (30 cm) long. Most of the absorption of food nutrients occurs here. The second and third sections, the jejunum and ileum, each measure about 10 feet (3 m) long. The small intestine curves under the large intestine and fills much of the abdominal cavity.

A 2-to-3-inch (5-to-7-cm) pouch, called the cecum, connects the small intestine to the large intestine. The entire large intestine, or colon, which is only about

6 feet (2 m) long, has a diameter of 2.5 inches (7 cm). It stores undigested food.

Vitamins and minerals are absorbed into the body from the large intestine. The body can also resorb 10 to 13.5 ounces (300 to 400 milliliters) of water from waste matter stored in the large intestine. The rectum, the final portion of the large intestine, ends in the anus.

Removing Bodily Waste

The body produces liquid and solid wastes. Liquid waste is filtered from the blood through the kidneys. It is stored in the bladder and eliminated as urine through the urethra. Kidneys also help regulate the volume of blood plasma and contribute to the body's ability to maintain a healthy blood pressure.

When whatever is left of your food reaches the large intestine, digestion is more or less complete. Solid wastes are then released as needed.

Eating Disorders

Some people suffer from eating disorders that can be life-threatening. *Anorexia nervosa* affects people who believe they are overweight. They starve themselves to become thinner. *Bulimia nervosa* victims gorge on huge amounts of food and then force themselves to vomit. Either of these disorders can seriously harm the victim's health.

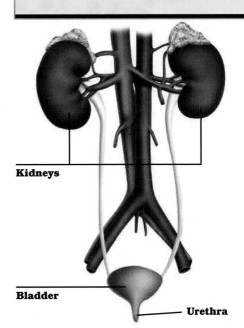

Kidneys

Bladder

Urethra

The kidneys, bladder, and urethra help the body eliminate liquid wastes.

7 A Network of Nerves

The human body sends messages to every muscle and every organ. Most messages are delivered along the internal circuits of the nervous system. The nervous system has two major parts: the central nervous system and the peripheral nervous system. A nerve consists of nerve fibers and connects to the central nervous system.

The central nervous system includes the brain and the spinal cord. As its name implies, it is the command center for the body. From gasping breaths to pounding heartbeats, itchy toes to fidgeting fingers, all human body systems depend on their connections to the brain. The nervous system works much like an electrical system.

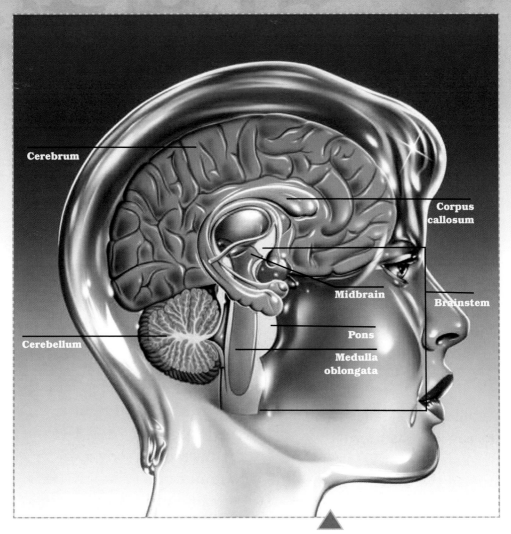

Cerebrum

Corpus callosum

Midbrain

Brainstem

Cerebellum

Pons

Medulla oblongata

The Brain

The human brain is divided into left and right hemispheres. The brain has three parts, the cerebrum, the cerebellum, and the brain stem. Each section of the brain controls a number of functions.

The cerebrum is the largest part of the brain. It controls sensory and motor (motion) control. When the

The human brain has distinct structures and areas that control different bodily processes.

Andreas Vesalius
(1514–1564)

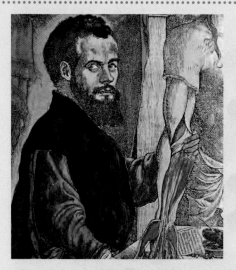

Vesalius was a Renaissance doctor. He was born in Belgium. Doctor Vesalius studied the anatomy of dead bodies of executed criminals. Vesalius published a series of books, *De humani corporis fabrica (On the Fabric of the Human Body)*, in 1542. These books included the first accurate descriptions of the skeleton, muscles, nervous system, blood vessels, and body organs.

body reacts to pain or jumps in the air, the cerebrum directs those movements. Speech, learning, reason, logic, and creativity are among the functions of the lobes of the cerebrum.

The cerebellum is located at the rear base of the brain. This area of the brain controls muscle coordination and motor activity. Walking, for example, requires that we have balance and use alternating muscle groups from our left and right legs. The cerebellum organizes the necessary body parts that allow us to walk. The cerebellum is also the center

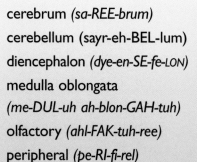

🔑 Pronunciation Key:

cerebrum *(sa-REE-brum)*
cerebellum *(sayr-eh-BEL-lum)*
diencephalon *(dye-en-SE-fe-LON)*
medulla oblongata
(me-DUL-uh ah-blon-GAH-tuh)
olfactory *(ahl-FAK-tuh-ree)*
peripheral *(pe-RI-fi-rel)*

for the sympathetic nervous system. It regulates all the internal organs.

The brainstem is the nerve tissue that connects the brain to the spinal cord. It includes several smaller parts, such as the medulla oblongata, the pons, and the areas called the midbrain and the diencephalon. The brainstem receives signals from the spinal cord and relays sensory and motor signals.

The Spinal Cord

The spinal cord is an 18-inch (45-cm) cord of nerve tissue running through a canal in the vertebral column. The bone cover protects the spinal cord from damage.

The outer portion of the spinal cord is white matter—nerve fibers covered by a sheath of white myelin. The center of the cord consists of gray nerve fibers. Three layers of protective membrane cover the entire cord. Thirty-one pairs of nerve roots extend

Addiction

Addiction is the result of abusing drugs or other substances, including hard drugs (cocaine, heroin), alcohol, tobacco, and certain prescription drugs. Addiction comes from repeated use of a substance until the body depends on having that substance. At first, the use of these substances gives the user a false sense of well-being or confidence. Repeated drug use turns into abuse when the body needs the substance to function.

from the spinal cord, forming the base of the peripheral nervous system.

In general, the spinal cord and nerve tissue has limited capacity to repair itself. That means spinal cord and nerve damage is usally permanent. Injuries to the spinal cord often result in paralysis of the legs and arms.

Sensory and Motor Nerves

The peripheral nervous system has several different types of nerves. Cranial nerves connect directly to the brain and include twelve pairs of nerves extending to facial muscles and glands. Spinal nerves are nerve roots that connect

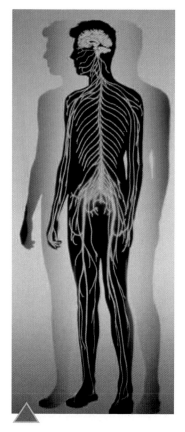

Nerves are the body's internal electrical wiring system.

to the spinal cord. Throughout the body, sensory fibers and motor fibers send impulses to the central nervous system.

For example, a sensory nerve can send a message to the brain about smelling a pizza. The sense of smell alerts the brain that something delicious is nearby. Other nerves may react to the smell by making the mouth water.

You can often control what your muscles are doing. The brain sends messages along nerves that travel to voluntary and involuntary muscles. This somatic nervous system causes muscles to react. A reflex is a spinal cord signal that does not involve the brain.

The autonomic nervous system works with involuntary muscles. It keeps your body working without you thinking about it. For instance, the autonomic nervous system "tells" the heart to start beating faster when you're scared, or puts your digestive system to work after a meal.

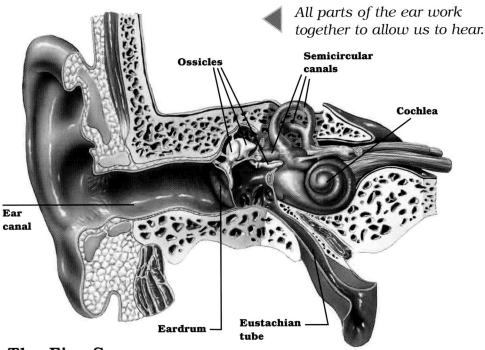

All parts of the ear work together to allow us to hear.

The Five Senses

The nervous system also controls our five senses: hearing, sight, smell, taste, and touch. In addition, the sense of equilibrium plays an important role in daily life.

Sound waves that enter the outer ear are funneled through the ear canal to the eardrum. The eardrum vibrates, which moves the tiniest bones in the body, the three ear ossicles. These transmit the sound vibrations to the inner ear.

There, inside a snail-shaped structure called the cochlea, tiny hairy cells deep inside the skull vibrate and transmit nerve impulses to the brain.

Hearing ability varies from person to person. Some people can hear a greater range of sound and higher or lower pitches than others. Other people can hear different volumes—from whisper quiet to very loud sounds.

It is important to note that any hearing damage caused

by exposure to loud noises is cumulative. That means that it adds up over time. Damage to the hairy cells deep inside the ear leads to permanent hearing loss.

The inner ear is also our center of equilibrium, or balance. An ear infection can affect our equilibrium in much the same way that being on a boat in rough seas throws us off balance.

The retina lines the rear of the eyeball. It works like a movie screen. The retina contains tiny cells called rods (light and motion receptors) and cones (color and detail receptors) that help us form an image when light enters the eye. The retina transmits impulses along the optic nerve, directly to the brain. The brain translates the message—*I see a dog . . . a rose . . . a balloon.* Because of the way light enters the eye and travels through the lens, we actually see everything

The lens focuses an image on the retina.

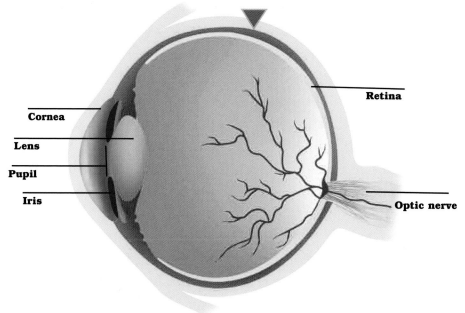

Cornea

Lens

Pupil

Iris

Retina

Optic nerve

upside down. Our brains flip the images right side up.

As air moves through the nasal cavity, our noses detect a variety of odors, such as frying onions, perfume, and freshly cut grass. This sense of smell is centered on a postage-stamp-sized bunch of olfactory cells that line the top of the nasal cavity.

Information about a specific scent travels along olfactory nerve fibers to the brain. Experience allows us to recognize an enormous variety of smells.

Taste is closely connected to smell. Both senses work together to make food appealing and to protect us from poisons and toxins. Taste buds cover our tongues. We can taste sweet, sour, salty, and bitter. The sense of taste is closely linked to the digestive system and the endocrine system.

When we smell and taste something delicious, our bodies react by releasing digestive juices and signaling the muscles of the digestive system to get to work.

The sense of touch reacts to pain, pressure, heat, cold, and vibration. Nerve endings in the skin, muscles, joints, and organs sense an outside stimulus and send a message to the brain.

Our sensory organs help us collect information about the world around us. Ultimately, however, our brain is what tells the body how to react.

Careers in Eye Care

There are several professions that provide eye care. Optometrists test vision, prescribe corrective lenses, and fit contact lenses. Ophthalmologists are medical doctors who specialize in eye health, diseases, and disorders. Ophthalmic surgeons operate on eyes to correct disorders or vision problems.

8 Hormones and Reproduction

The endocrine system produces chemical messengers called hormones that are released directly into the bloodstream. Hormones help regulate metabolism by sending messages that tell the body when and how to work, change, and grow. Hormones also make us blush.

Glands in the body secrete hormones. They travel through the entire body, but only affect specific cells. Those cells "read" and react to the hormonal message. The body produces dozens of different hormones. Each has a specific job that keeps the body's metabolism functioning properly.

Major hormone-producing glands include the pituitary, thyroid, pancreas, adrenals, testes (male),

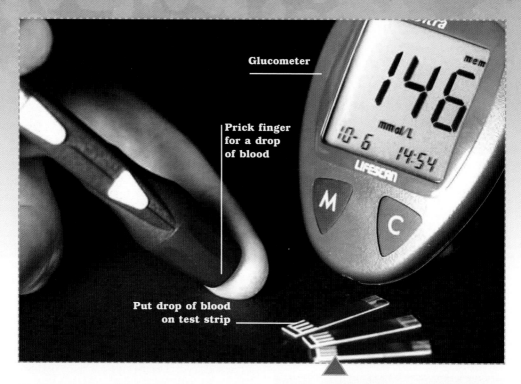

Glucometer

Prick finger
for a drop
of blood

Put drop of blood
on test strip

and ovaries (female). Each gland produces a number of different hormones with specific tasks. Many hormones are produced and used daily. Others are only needed during certain circumstances.

Insulin, a hormone that helps the body metabolize food, is continuously produced in the pancreas. Prolactin, secreted from the pituitary gland, stimulates milk production in women immediately after they have given birth.

The body needs an even balance of hormones. If too much or too little of a specific hormone is produced, a problem occurs. For example, the

Diabetics must test their blood sugar level regularly. A pinprick of blood is dabbed onto a test strip. The strip is inserted into the glucometer, which gives a blood sugar level reading. A reading above 126 indicates that the person being tested has diabetes.

pituitary gland produces the
human growth hormone. This
hormone activates the body's
normal growth. Too little
human growth hormone
during childhood produces
dwarfism while too much
results in gigantism.

Reproductive Systems
One of the major functions
of hormones is to activate the
reproductive systems of males

Pronunciation Key:

diabetes *(DIE-uh-BEE-tees)*
pancreas *(PAN-kree-us)*
pituitary *(pe-TWO-uh-TAYR-ee)*
testes *(TES-tees)*

and females. This portion of
the life cycle is called puberty.
When a male reaches his early
teens, his body enters puberty.
The testes begin secreting
more testosterone, which tells
the body to mature. The male
grows taller and gains more
muscle. His voice deepens.
More body hair begins to grow.
The male sex organs, which
include the testicles, seminal
vesicles, and prostate gland,
are located internally and
externally. These undergo
metabolic and size changes.

Most girls reach puberty
slighlty earlier than males,
between the ages of ten and
fourteen. The female reproductive
system includes the ovaries,
fallopian tubes, and uterus.
These organs lie entirely inside
the body. Mature ovaries

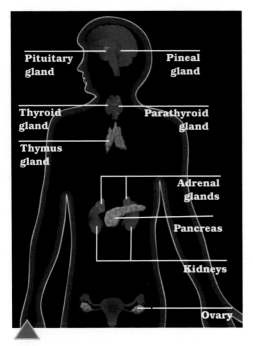

*Glands secrete hormones that
control metabolism and other
bodily functions.*

measure about 1.5 to 2 inches (4 to 5 cm). Ovaries secrete the hormones estrogen and progesterone that trigger changes in the female body. Females soon begin a monthly hormone cycle in which the ovaries alternately release one mature egg, or ovum.

The egg must be fertlized before it develops into a new human being. Fertilization occurs in the fallopian tube. During fertilization, about 500 million sperm travel to the female's body. Only one sperm actually fertilizes an egg. At that instant, the egg's membrane changes to prevent any other sperm from entering. The fertilized egg is now called a zygote. It floats down the fallopian tube, implants in the uterine wall, and becomes an embryo. Two months later, it becomes a fetus. Nine months after fertilization, a baby is born.

A human embryo undergoes a series of changes as it develops inside its mother in nine months.

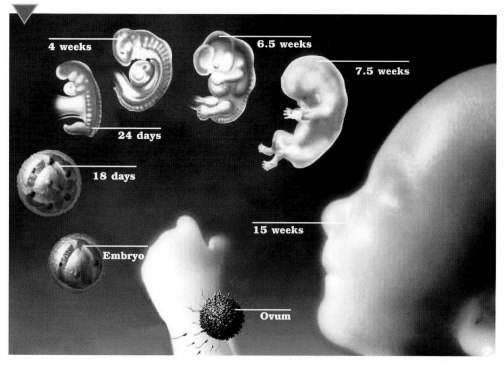

4 weeks

6.5 weeks

7.5 weeks

24 days

18 days

15 weeks

Embryo

Ovum

Glossary

autonomic refers to body processes that are not under conscious control of the individual, such as heart rate, breathing, or secretion of hormones and enzymes

capillaries minute blood vessels that interlace the tissues; can function as either arteries or veins

cardiac related to the heart

chromosomes any of several threadlike bodies, consisting of chromatin, that appear during cell division to carry the genes in a linear order

circulatory moving or passing around within a closed system; often refers to the heart and all its vessels

cytoplasm a gel-like substance that forms the body of a cell

deoxyribonucleic acid (DNA) a long-chain nuclear compound that carries genetic information

diaphragm a flat muscle that separates the thoracic cavity from the abdominal cavity

duodenum the first portion of the small intestine

emphysema a serious lung disease often caused by smoking; occurs when alveoli break down to form large air pockets in lungs

endocrine relating to glands that secrete directly into tissues or the bloodstream

enzymes a group of naturally produced proteins that help the body work properly, such as pepsin in the stomach used for digestion

epiglottis a flap of tissue at the base of the throat that covers the opening to the trachea when swallowing

equilibrium a sense of balance

esophagus a muscular tube that connects the mouth with the stomach and moves food along through muscular contractions called peristalsis

excretory relating to getting rid of bodily wastes

fallopian tubes that connect ovaries to the uterus

gastric having to do with the stomach

genetic relating to genes and heredity

glands organs that produce and release chemical substances

intestines long, tubular abdominal organs that absorb nutrients and store waste

involuntary working without the person's consious control

ligament a thick, fibrous band of connective tissue that connects bone to bone

marrow a soft, fatty tissue in the interior cavities of bones that is a major site of blood cell production

myelin a whitish material made of proteins and fats that surrounds the spinal cord and some nerve cells

olfactory having to do with the sense of smell

organelles tiny, specialized cell components with their own particular function, for example, ribosomes or mitochondria

peripheral on the outer edges of a system, such as the foot nerves of the nervous system

peristalsis the progressive, involuntary wave of contraction and relaxation of a tubular muscular system that moves contents through the system

platelets small cell fragments in the blood that aid in clotting

respiratory relating to the lungs or breathing process

somatic of—or relating to—body organs or limbs

sympathetic nervous system a part of the autonomic nervous system that prepares the body for action during stress and physical activity

tendon thick, fibrous connective tissue that connects a muscle to bone or to another body part

zygote the cell resulting from the union of an ovum and a sperm; the earliest stage after fertilization and before implantation. The zygote becomes an embryo once it undergoes cell division after implantation.

For More Information

Books

Glass, Susan. *The Circulatory System: The Human Body*. Essentials in Science (series). Perfection Learning (2004).

Graham, Sue, Editor. *1001 Facts About the Human Body*. Backpack Books (series). DK Publishing (2002).

Gray, Susan Heinrichs. *The Muscular System*. Body systems (series). Child's World (2003).

Human Body. Eyewitness Books (series). DK children (2004).

Newquist, H. P. *The Great Brain Book: An Inside Look at the Inside of Your Head*. Scholastic (2005).

Parker, Steven. *Brain, Nerves, and Senses. Digestion and Reproduction. Heart, Blood, and Lungs. Skin, Muscles, and Bones*. Understanding the Human Body (series). Gareth Stevens (2005).

Snedden, Robert. *Cell Division & Genetics*. Cells & Life (series). Heinemann (2002).

Web Sites

www.lung.ca/children/index_kids.html
Choose your grade level and explore the respiratory system.

http://uimc.discoveryhospital.com/shared/Anatomy/default2.htm
Click on "guided tours" to learn about different body systems.

http://vilenski.org/science/humanbody
Visit this site for an interactive adventure through the human body.

www.medtropolis.com/VBody.asp
Listen and learn about the human body through this interactive presentation.

www.kidshealth.org/kid/body/mybody.html
Surf the KidsHealth site for a variety of links to human body information.

Publisher's note to educators and parents: Our editors have carefully reviewed these Web sites to ensure that they are suitable for children. Many Web sites change frequently, however, and we cannot guarantee that a site's future contents will continue to meet our high standards of quality and educational value. Be advised that children should be closely supervised whenever they access the Internet.

Index